Francis Frith's
NORTH DEVON COAST

PHOTOGRAPHIC MEMORIES

Francis Frith's
NORTH DEVON COAST

◆

John Bainbridge

First published in the United Kingdom in 2000 by
Frith Book Company Ltd

Text and Design copyright © Frith Book Company Ltd
Photographs copyright © The Francis Frith Collection

British Library Cataloguing in Publication Data

North Devon Coast
John Bainbridge
ISBN 1-85937-146-9

Frith Book Company Ltd
Frith's Barn, Teffont,
Salisbury, Wiltshire SP3 5QP
Tel: +44 (0) 1722 716 376
Email: info@frithbook.co.uk
www.frithbook.co.uk

Printed and bound in Great Britain

Front Cover: **Bideford, The Promenade 1919** 69331

Contents

FRANCIS FRITH: *Victorian Pioneer*

FRANCIS FRITH, Victorian founder of the world-famous photographic archive, was a complex and fascinating man. A devout Quaker and a highly successful Victorian businessman, he was both philosophic by nature and pioneering in outlook.

By 1855 Francis Frith had already established a wholesale grocery business in Liverpool, and sold it for the astonishing sum of £200,000, which is the equivalent today of over £15,000,000. Now a multi-millionaire, he was able to indulge his passion for travel. As a child he had pored over travel books written by early explorers, and his fancy and imagination had been stirred by family holidays to the sublime mountain regions of Wales and Scotland. 'What a land of spirit-stirring and enriching scenes and places!' he had written. He was to return to these scenes of grandeur in later years to 'recapture the thousands of vivid and tender memories', but with a different purpose. Now in his thirties, and captivated by the new science of photography, Frith set out on a series of pioneering journeys to the Nile regions that occupied him from 1856 until 1860.

INTRIGUE AND ADVENTURE

He took with him on his travels a specially-designed wicker carriage that acted as both dark-room and sleeping chamber. These far-flung journeys were packed with intrigue and adventure. In his life story, written when he was sixty-three, Frith tells of being held captive by bandits, and of fighting 'an awful midnight battle to the very point of surrender with a deadly pack of hungry, wild dogs'. Sporting flowing Arab costume, Frith arrived at Akaba by camel seventy years before Lawrence, where he encountered 'desert princes and rival sheikhs, blazing with jewel-hilted swords'.

During these extraordinary adventures he was assiduously exploring the desert regions bordering the Nile and patiently recording the antiquities and peoples with his camera. He was the first photographer to venture beyond the sixth cataract. Africa was still the mysterious 'Dark Continent', and Stanley and Livingstone's historic meeting was a decade into the future. The conditions for picture taking confound belief. He laboured for hours in his wicker dark-room in the sweltering heat of the desert, while the volatile chemicals fizzed dangerously in their trays. Often he was forced to work in remote tombs and caves where conditions were cooler. Back in London he exhibited his photographs and was 'rapturously cheered' by members of the Royal Society. His reputation as a photographer was made overnight. An eminent modern historian has likened their impact on the population of the time to that on our own generation of the first photographs taken on the surface of the moon.

VENTURE OF A LIFE-TIME

Characteristically, Frith quickly spotted the opportunity to create a new business as a specialist publisher of photographs. He lived in an era of immense and sometimes violent change. For the poor in the early part of Victoria's reign work was a drudge and the hours long, and people had precious little free time to enjoy themselves.

Most had no transport other than a cart or gig at their disposal, and had not travelled far beyond the boundaries of their own town or village. However, by the 1870s, the railways had threaded their way across the country, and Bank Holidays and half-day Saturdays had been made obligatory by Act of Parliament. All of a sudden the ordinary working man and his family were able to enjoy days out and see a little more of the world.

With characteristic business acumen, Francis Frith foresaw that these new tourists would enjoy having souvenirs to commemorate their days out. In 1860 he married Mary Ann Rosling and set out with the intention of photographing every city, town and village in Britain. For the next thirty years he travelled the country by train and by pony and trap, producing fine photographs of seaside resorts and beauty spots that were keenly bought by millions of Victorians. These prints were painstakingly pasted into family albums and pored over during the dark nights of winter, rekindling precious memories of summer excursions.

THE RISE OF FRITH & CO

Frith's studio was soon supplying retail shops all over the country. To meet the demand he gathered about him a small team of photographers, and published the work of independent artist-photographers of the calibre of Roger Fenton and Francis Bedford. In order to gain some understanding of the scale of Frith's business one only has to look at the catalogue issued by Frith & Co in 1886: it runs to some 670

pages, listing not only many thousands of views of the British Isles but also many photographs of most European countries, and China, Japan, the USA and Canada – note the sample page shown above from the hand-written *Frith & Co* ledgers detailing pictures taken. By 1890 Frith had created the greatest specialist photographic publishing company in the world, with over 2,000 outlets – more than the combined number that Boots and WH Smith have today! The picture on the right shows the *Frith & Co* display board at Ingleton in the Yorkshire Dales. Beautifully constructed with mahogany frame and gilt inserts, it could display up to a dozen local scenes.

POSTCARD BONANZA

◆

The ever-popular holiday postcard we know today took many years to develop. In 1870 the Post Office issued the first plain cards, with a pre-printed stamp on one face. In 1894 they allowed other publishers' cards to be sent through the mail with an attached adhesive halfpenny stamp. Demand grew rapidly, and in 1895 a new size of postcard was permitted called the

court card, but there was little room for illustration. In 1899, a year after Frith's death, a new card measuring 5.5 x 3.5 inches became the standard format, but it was not until 1902 that the divided back came into being, with address and message on one face and a full-size illustration on the other. *Frith & Co* were in the vanguard of postcard development, and Frith's sons Eustace and Cyril continued their father's monumental task, expanding the number of views offered to the public and recording more and more places in Britain, as the coasts and countryside were opened up to mass travel.

Francis Frith died in 1898 at his villa in Cannes, his great project still growing. The archive he created continued in business for another seventy years. By 1970 it contained over a third of a million pictures of 7,000 cities, towns and villages. The massive photographic record Frith has left to us stands as a living monument to a special and very remarkable man.

Frith's Archive: *A Unique Legacy*

FRANCIS FRITH'S legacy to us today is of immense significance and value, for the magnificent archive of evocative photographs he created provides a unique record of change in 7,000 cities, towns and villages throughout Britain over a century and more. Frith and his fellow studio photographers revisited locations many times down the years to update their views, compiling for us an enthralling and colourful pageant of British life and character.

We tend to think of Frith's sepia views of Britain as nostalgic, for most of us use them to conjure up memories of places in our own lives with which we have family associations. It often makes us forget that to Francis Frith they were records of daily life as it was actually being lived in the cities, towns and villages of his day. The Victorian age was one of great and often bewildering change for ordinary people, and though the pictures evoke an impression of slower times, life was as busy and hectic as it is today.

We are fortunate that Frith was a photographer of the people, dedicated to recording the minutiae of everyday life. For it is this sheer wealth of visual data, the painstaking chronicle of changes in dress, transport, street layouts, buildings, housing, engineering and landscape that captivates us so much today. His remarkable images offer us a powerful link with the past and with the lives of our ancestors.

TODAY'S TECHNOLOGY

Computers have now made it possible for Frith's many thousands of images to be accessed almost instantly. In the Frith archive today, each photograph is carefully 'digitised' then stored on a CD Rom. Frith archivists can locate a single photograph amongst thousands within seconds. Views can be catalogued and sorted under a variety of categories of place and content to the immediate benefit of researchers. Inexpensive reference prints can be created for them at the touch of a mouse button, and a wide range of books and other printed materials assembled and published for a wider, more general readership - in the next twelve months over a hundred Frith local history titles will be published! The

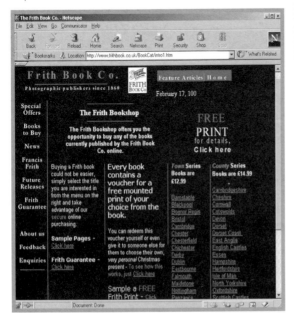

See Frith at www. frithbook.co.uk

day-to-day workings of the archive are very different from how they were in Francis Frith's time: imagine the herculean task of sorting through eleven tons of glass negatives as Frith had to do to locate a particular sequence of pictures! Yet the archive still prides itself on maintaining the same high standards of excellence laid down by Francis Frith, including the painstaking cataloguing and indexing of every view.

It is curious to reflect on how the internet now allows researchers in America and elsewhere greater instant access to the archive than Frith himself ever enjoyed. Many thousands of individual views can be called up on screen within seconds on one of the Frith internet sites, enabling people living continents away to revisit the streets of their ancestral home town, or view places in Britain where they have enjoyed holidays. Many overseas researchers welcome the chance to view special theme selections, such as transport, sports, costume and ancient monuments.

We are certain that Francis Frith would have heartily approved of these modern developments, for he himself was always working at the very limits of Victorian photographic technology.

THE VALUE OF THE ARCHIVE TODAY

Because of the benefits brought by the computer, Frith's images are increasingly studied by social historians, by researchers into genealogy and ancestory, by architects, town planners, and by teachers and schoolchildren involved in local history projects. In addition, the archive offers every one of us a unique opportunity to examine the places where we and our families have lived and worked down the years. Immensely successful in Frith's own era, the archive is now, a century and more on, entering a new phase of popularity.

THE PAST IN TUNE WITH THE FUTURE

Historians consider the Francis Frith Collection to be of prime national importance. It is the only archive of its kind remaining in private ownership and has been valued at a million pounds. However, this figure is now rapidly increasing as digital technology enables more and more people around the world to enjoy its benefits.

Francis Frith's archive is now housed in an historic timber barn in the beautiful village of Teffont in Wiltshire. Its founder would not recognize the archive office as it is today. In place of the many thousands of dusty boxes containing glass plate negatives and an all-pervading odour of photographic chemicals, there are now ranks of computer screens. He would be amazed to watch his images travelling round the world at unimaginable speeds through network and internet lines.

The archive's future is both bright and exciting. Francis Frith, with his unshakeable belief in making photographs available to the greatest number of people, would undoubtedly approve of what is being done today with his lifetime's work. His photographs, depicting our shared past, are now bringing pleasure and enlightenment to millions around the world a century and more after his death.

NORTH DEVON COAST
The Country of Two Rivers

IT WAS PROBABLY the novelist Henry Williamson who first described the countryside around the Taw and Torridge as the Country of the Two Rivers. Williamson certainly immortalised this intriguing landscape of golden sands and swirling tidal waters in a series of memorable novels, such as the famous 'Tarka the Otter' and several collections of country essays. Much of this part of North Devon is now called Tarka Country in tribute to the author's most famous creation. The railway line from Exeter to Barnstaple is now called the Tarka Line, and walkers and cyclists can follow the Tarka Trail - a long-distance pathway that follows much of the route taken by that fictional creature.

This may all sound like tourist board wishful thinking, but in fact it reflects the unique character of this area. Henry Williamson observed and interpreted this land in a way that no writer had ever done before. It served him well as a backdrop not only for his animal stories and nature notes, but as the scene of his two long novel sequences 'The Flax of Dream' and 'A Chronicle of Ancient Sunlight'. Williamson came to North Devon, shell-shocked and exhausted, after service in the First World War, and discovered, as many have done before and since, the healing power of the quiet fields and woods, and the drama of its coastline. To read his descriptions of places like Braunton Burrows, Saunton Sands and the coastline beyond Croyde is to gain a deeper appreciation of this often subtle terrain.

Most visitors find themselves at some time in North Devon's two major towns, Barnstaple and Bideford. Barnstaple, or Barum, lies at the end of the railway line, a gateway to a wild frontier. It is the market town par excellence and many Devonians make regular trips there to the famous pannier market - in fact the whole of Devon seems to be there on busy days. Its stalls are a colourful delight, for virtually anything can be bought there, and the pubs and restaurants sell delicious food.

Bideford is a seaport of ancient fame. It was from here that many of Queen Elizabeth's sea-dogs set out on their expeditions around the globe. Not all returned. Sir Richard

Grenville's 'Revenge', crewed mostly by Bideford men, went down with all guns blazing in an unequal battle with fifteen vessels of the Spanish war fleet. Walking along Bideford's quayside or strolling across the twenty-four arched bridge over the Torridge, you can almost see in your imagination these old sailing ships setting out. Those old sailors would have heard the cry of the gulls and smelt the salt tang blowing in off the estuary, and watched the green hilltops get further and further away as they sailed down the river.

It is unfair to single out just one of the smaller towns, but Appledore is a lovely place to stay if you want peace and quiet. Not that the tourists don't come. They do, but this little town lacks the larger population of Barnstaple and Bideford. Appledore, with those narrow streets that so attract the artistic eye, is like a little bit of Cornwall transported to Devon. The Tudor topographer Leland described Appledore as 'a good village'. It still is, and all the better for being a working community.

Visiting the Country of the Two Rivers and comparing the photographs with what may be seen today is an interesting exercise, particularly if you have already discovered it in your imagination by studying the writings of North Devon's famous author, Henry Williamson. And, after a long absence, even the otters have returned to the waters of the Taw and Torridge.

INSTOW, THE FORESHORE 1919 69337

APPLEDORE, BUDE STREET 1906 55967
The narrow streets of Appledore are more reminiscent of some of the coastal towns of Cornwall than anywhere else in Devon. Wherever you go you can smell the salt tang of the estuary of the Two Rivers and the sea beyond.

APPLEDORE, THE QUAY 1907 59305
Appledore has long been famed for its shipbuilding industry. Several replica sailing ships have been built here, including the 'Nonsuch' - the famous Hudson's Bay trader.

APPLEDORE, THE QUAY 1923 75148
The Welsh steamer 'Plas Dinam' from Aberystwyth sets out from Appledore Quay. The close proximity of North Devon to Wales meant there was a constant trade between the ports on either side of the Bristol Channel.

APPLEDORE
The Quay 1923 75145
This is a splendid portrait of Appledore's quayside, with fishermen travelling out to their boats and a party of tourists being taken out for a boating trip. Times were hard for all Devon ports in the 1920s, after the profitable times of Queen Victoria's reign.

APPLEDORE, WEST QUAY 1924 75149

APPLEDORE
West Quay 1924
Legend tells us that the Danish warrior Hubba and his hordes landed on this side of the estuary during the reign of Alfred the Great. This Viking raider fell in battle after a confrontation with the Saxon army, who captured his precious Raven Banner.

◆

APPLEDORE
Bude Street 1930
Every artist and photographer loves the narrow streets of Appledore. According to the Anglo-Saxon Chronicle, a village called Tawmouth stood on this site a thousand years ago.

APPLEDORE, BUDE STREET 1930 83496

APPLEDORE, BUDE STREET 1930 83497
Leland, that well-travelled topographic chronicler, visited Appledore in 1540, describing the place as 'a good village'. Elizabethan sailors recognised the importance of the broad estuary as a good strategic anchorage.

APPLEDORE, MARKET STREET 1930 83499
This old town has supported many trades throughout its long history; some legitimate, such as shipbuilding and salmon-netting, others less respectable, including piracy and smuggling. These old street patterns have changed very little since those stirring times.

APPLEDORE, THE QUAY c1955 A55010
By the 1950s, the salmon-netting had declined with the reduction in fish-stocks, but the estuary had become a popular place for leisure boating. The estuary of the Two Rivers is not the easiest place to sail, being beset with strong currents and sandbanks, but it provides a worthy challenge for the skilled yachtsman.

APPLEDORE, FROM INSTOW c1955 A55019
A car ferry crosses the river Torridge from Instow to Appledore. This photograph shows how closely the residents of Appledore live to the estuary and the sea. Beyond the town is the sandy ridge of Northam Burrows.

APPLEDORE, THE QUAY c1955 A55023

Two ships, one Welsh, the other from Bristol, are moored at Appledore Quay. The town looks quiet, but it was about to experience a resurgence of its shipbuilding trade.

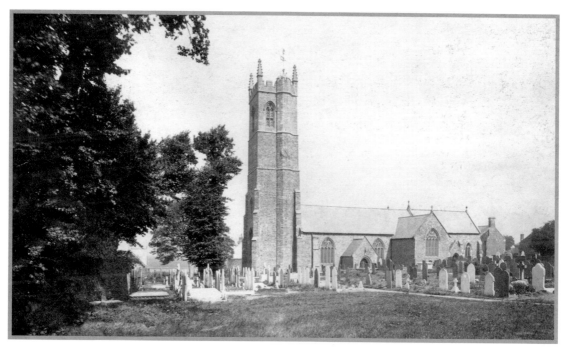

NORTHAM, THE CHURCH 1890 24833

There are few statelier church towers in Devon than this splendid structure at Northam, the haunt of seagulls and rooks. It has long served as a landmark for shipping coming in over the bar at the estuary's mouth.

NORTHAM
The Village 1890 24835

This is Northam as the Victorian novelist Charles Kingsley would have known it at the time he was writing his novel 'Westward Ho!' Kingsley's hero Amyas Leigh was fictional, but many real life members of the Leigh family are buried in the churchyard.

NORTHAM, BONE HILL 1906 55977
An Edwardian lady takes a baby for an outing in its perambulator. Taking the sea air was a favourite recreation for young and old. Edwardians believed that the ozone around Northam Burrows was especially beneficial to good health.

NORTHAM, THE VILLAGE 1907 59300

Children play in the square at Northam, all wearing hats as polite fashion demanded. Two of the youngsters are riding a most unusual tricycle.

NORTHAM, THE CHURCH 1919 69346

This is a fine study of Northam church. Northam stands on what is effectively a long peninsula between the River Torridge and the sea. There has been more building since these photographs were taken, but the village remains unspoiled.

NORTHAM, THE VILLAGE 1919 64347
A view of a quiet street in Northam soon after the First World War. The poster on the corner shop advertises the 'Church of England Missionary Society Exhibition and Sale of Work'.

NORTHAM, THE SQUARE c1955 N37011
The 1950s saw the advent of the age of popular motoring. Parking in Northam's streets is not now the easy undertaking it was half a century ago. The sign on the telegraph pole says 'Queue Here for Westward Ho!'

BIDEFORD, THE BRIDGE 1890 24792
Bideford lies a little further up the Torridge from Northam. In its day Bideford was a port of great importance, though its fortunes as a maritime centre declined in the last century. Here a young boy rests after helping with the harvest.

BIDEFORD, THE QUAY 1890 24800
Bideford was the greatest Elizabethan sea port in Devon after Plymouth. From here sailed many of Queen Elizabeth's sea-dogs, such as Drake, Grenville, Hawkins and Frobisher.

BIDEFORD, OLD FORD FARM 1890 24806
Agriculture and the sea dictated the fortunes of most Devon seaside towns in days gone by. In this photograph of a late-Victorian farm, we see a working agricultural holding as it really was - a far cry from the romantic view of Victorian farming life seen so frequently in films and on television programmes.

BIDEFORD, THE TOWN AND BRIDGE 1899 43075
Bideford's twenty-four arched bridge has spanned the Torridge for seven hundred years. The span of the arches varies between 12 and 25 feet. Bideford, as its name suggests, stands near to a more ancient crossing point on the Torridge - the place 'by-the-ford'.

BIDEFORD, ACROSS THE RIVER 1899 43077
Bideford was given to the Grenville family by King William Rufus, remaining in their possession until the year 1744. One of the family, Sir Richard Grenville, was the sailor and navigator, and another Sir Richard was the King's General in the West during the English Civil War.

BIDEFORD, THE BRIDGE FROM THE RAILWAY STATION 1899 43079
Sir Richard Grenville's ship 'Revenge' was crewed by Bideford men on its last fateful voyage in 1591. The gallant Sir Richard was mortally wounded when his ship fought a lone battle against fifteen Spanish vessels.

BIDEFORD, THE PROMENADE 1906 55925

These two photographs show how quickly new forms of transport can take over the streets of a town in the space of a few years.

BIDEFORD, THE PROMENADE 1919 69331

Motoring opened up the North Devon countryside in a way that would have seemed unimaginable to earlier generations of visitor.

BIDEFORD, BRIDGE STREET 1906 55933

BIDEFORD
Bridge Street 1906

One former resident of Bideford, Mary Sexton, is immortalised by a much-quoted epitaph in the churchyard: 'Here lies the body of Mary Sexton, Who pleased many a man, But never vex'd one; Not like the woman under the next stone'.

◆

BIDEFORD
High Street c1955

By the 1950s car parking was becoming something of a problem in the High Street on busy days. The difficulties of finding somewhere to leave a car was alleviated by the introduction of car parks - taken for granted now, but not that common half a century ago.

BIDEFORD, HIGH STREET c1955 B90040

INSTOW, THE FORESHORE 1919 69337
Going back up the eastern side of the Torridge we come to Instow, on the opposite bank to Appledore. Instow is really two discrete communities in origin, one by the river, which served the fishing community, and another inland, an older agricultural settlement. Here some locals sit on the bank of the Torridge and pose for the photographer.

INSTOW
The Quay 1919

Instow is situated on a broad cape where the Torridge meets her sister river the Taw in a broad and magnificent estuary; a haunt of wild birds and bobbing fishing boats. The salmon-netting trade has declined now almost to extinction, but recreational yachting is providing an alternative use for the old port.

◆

INSTOW
Paddling 1919

What is a seaside holiday in North Devon without a few hours beachcombing?

INSTOW, THE QUAY 1919 69339

INSTOW, PADDLING 1919 69343

INSTOW, ON THE BEACH 1919 69344

INSTOW, THE VILLAGE 1919 69345

INSTOW
On the Beach 1919
These youngsters are having a happy time exploring the pools and shallows of the Taw and Torridge estuary.

◆

INSTOW
The Village 1919
Much of the parish church of St John the Baptist is 12th-century in origin, though there are some earlier Norman remains, including the font. A north aisle was added in 1547 by Richard Waterman and his wife Emma. There is a memorial inside the building to the 18th-century botanist Humphrey Sibthorp, professor at Oxford University.

INSTOW, GENERAL VIEW c1955 I14001

Here we have a view over Instow, Appledore and the estuary, with the sand dunes of Northam and Braunton Burrows beyond. The number of yachts seen here indicates the popularity of the sport around the North Devon coast.

INSTOW, THE RAILWAY c1955 I14002

The coming of the railway brought many more visitors into this hitherto isolated region, particularly during the 20th century when the opportunity to afford a seaside holiday became more widely available.

INSTOW, THE POST OFFICE AND THE QUAY c1955 114017

Instow became a resort during the early years of the last century, attracting a clientele that liked to explore the lonely reaches of the estuary and the beauty of a wild and rugged coastline.

FREMINGTON, THE CHURCH c1955 F100001

St Peter's Church at Fremington suffered badly at the hands of Victorian restorers, though it was not as thoroughly ruined as some guidebook writers like to suggest. Its lych gate is rather an attractive structure, seen at its best in this photograph.

FREMINGTON, MAIN ROAD c1955 F100002

Fremington became a suburb of Barnstaple in the last century, and became rather blighted with overspill development. But some older buildings have survived in the shadow of the church wall. The village pubs remain an attraction for the passing motorist.

FREMINGTON, THE VILLAGE c1955 F100006
Fremington lies just inland from the Taw estuary and was formerly a minor port. There were some small industries here too, notably potteries working the local clay.

FREMINGTON, THE VILLAGE c1955 F100007
Fremington has suffered from being on the main road between Barnstaple and Instow. Its streets nowadays are never quite as peaceful as they seem to be in this and the next photograph.

FREMINGTON, THE VILLAGE c1955 F100009
But a walk into the combes and hillsides south of the village brings the rambler into quieter countryside with superb view over the estuary.

BARNSTAPLE, THE PROMENADE 1890 24860
Barnstaple is situated at the head of the Taw estuary and is North Devon's largest town. Like Bideford, its gets its name from the location of an ancient ford, which was once marked by a staple or post.

BARNSTAPLE, FROM THE RAILWAY STATION 1894 33413

Barnstaple is one of the oldest boroughs in England, and minted its own coins a thousand years ago. Tradition alleges that King Athelstan gave the town its first charter, though there is no historical evidence for this. Barnstaple did, however, belong to Edward the Confessor and later William the Conqueror at the time of Domesday.

BARNSTAPLE, HIGH STREET 1894 33422

Barnstaple features a great deal in the history of English literature. Shakespeare may have performed here on a tour with his acting company. The diarist Samuel Pepys certainly visited, for it was here that he courted his wife. But the town's most renowned son was the playwright and satirist John Gay, author of 'The Beggar's Opera', who was born here in 1685.

BARNSTAPLE, HIGH STREET 1903 49620

BARNSTAPLE
High Street 1903
'The Beggar's Opera' brought Gay both fame and wealth; its blend of satire, colour and melody achieved an almost unprecedented theatrical long run. Barnstaple's poet now lies buried in Westminster Abbey.

◆

BARNSTAPLE
The Almshouses 1903
Barnstaple was a major trading centre from medieval times; until the development of Torbay, it was Devon's third town after Exeter and Plymouth. The town's wealth helped to pay for measures to alleviate poverty, such as these almshouses.

BARNSTAPLE, THE ALMSHOUSES 1903 49625

BARNSTAPLE, THE SQUARE 1903 49616
Barnstaple's Square contains an impressive memorial to Prince Albert, Consort to Queen Victoria.

BARNSTAPLE, THE SQUARE 1912 64564
Even into the reigns of Edward VII and George V, horse transport dominated the streets of the town, although, as this photograph shows, a motor garage and signposting had appeared.

BARNSTAPLE, THE SQUARE 1935 86654

By 1935 Prideux's motor garage was still in business, but the kiosk in the previous photographs had disappeared - perhaps because of the danger from the motor cars that had now taken over this busy street. One wonders whether the man painting the bollard on the traffic island was any relation to the small boy seen leaning on that very same post in 1912?

BARNSTAPLE, BOUTPORT STREET 1919 69322

By the end of the First World War, passers-by - familiar with photography - no longer stared at the cameraman as their forebears did in previous decades. Many of the people in this picture had probably indulged in the fast-growing hobby of picture-taking by this time.

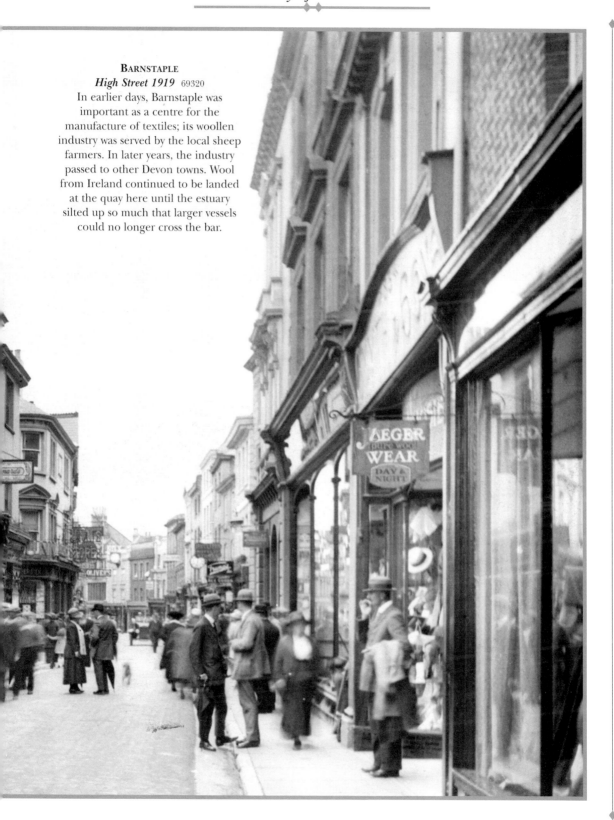

BARNSTAPLE
High Street 1919 69320
In earlier days, Barnstaple was important as a centre for the manufacture of textiles; its woollen industry was served by the local sheep farmers. In later years, the industry passed to other Devon towns. Wool from Ireland continued to be landed at the quay here until the estuary silted up so much that larger vessels could no longer cross the bar.

BARNSTAPLE, THE STRAND, HORSE FAIR 1923 75164

Barnstaple's great fair is held in September and lasts for five days. But there are smaller fairs and markets for livestock and other commodities. The town's weekly Pannier Market, with its many delightful stalls, attracts visitors from right across Devon.

BARNSTAPLE, HIGH STREET CORNER 1935 86657

Here we see a policeman on point duty in the first half of the 20th century, in itself an activity that has been more or less relegated to the history books. The Royal and Fortescue Hotel, formerly the Fortescue Arms, is one of Barnstaple's oldest hotels.

BISHOPS TAWTON, THE VILLAGE 1890 24886

The spire of Bishops Tawton church is a familiar sight to the traveller journeying from Exeter to Barnstaple. The church has several monuments to the Chichester family, who have owned land in the vicinity for hundreds of years. A modern descendant was the round-the-world yachtsman Sir Francis Chichester.

BISHOPS TAWTON, BARNSTAPLE ROAD c1960 B105003

Early bishops of Exeter lived here from Saxon times until the reign of Henry VIII, and some of the ruins of their Palace can be seen near to the church. In recent years Bishops Tawton has become something of a dormitory community for nearby Barnstaple.

LANDKEY, THE CHURCH c1885 L193301

LANDKEY
The Church c1885
This is an idyllic portrait of a parish church and its surroundings in Queen Victoria's time, a world away from the technological pressures of the 21st century. Landkey's 15th-century church tower is the most prominent landmark in this broad valley. This church was fortunate in escaping the worst excesses of the Victorian ecclesiastical restorers.

◆

LANDKEY
Barnstaple Road c1955
The Aclands, one of Devon's leading families in past times, took their name from Ackland Barton, near to Landkey, during the time of the Plantagenet kings. Sir Richard Acland finally sold the manor to his tenant in 1945.

LANDKEY, BARNSTAPLE ROAD c1955 L193011

GOODLEIGH, THE VILLAGE 1894 33425

The Aclands also lived at Goodleigh, and there are Acland monuments in the village church, which stands on high ground above some very pretty cottages. Much of the church has been rebuilt, but it still holds much interest as a typical Devon place of worship.

GOODLEIGH, THE CHURCH 1894 33426

Goodleigh lies north-east of Barnstaple, just far enough away to have avoided being swamped by its sprawling neighbour. It was and still remains a good area for sheep farming. In more prosperous times its wool helped supply the Barnstaple textile market.

BRAUNTON, GENERAL VIEW 1900 45680

In the Dark Ages the missionary Saint Brannoc was told in a dream that he must build a chapel at the first place on his journey that he met with a sow and her piglets. The prophecy was fulfilled here, and Braunton was named in the saint's honour.

BRAUNTON, THE VILLAGE 1900 45679

Braunton has grown considerably since this photograph was taken, almost certainly because of its nearness to Barnstaple. The centre of the parish remains much the same, however, and would be easily recognised by the Frith photographer.

BRAUNTON, CHURCH STREET 1900 45684

To the south-west of Braunton is the Great Field, a survival of the medieval open field system of agriculture, where farmers worked unenclosed strips of land in the same field. As many as 85 farmers worked the Field at the beginning of the last century, but there are now only a few left.

BRAUNTON, OLD HOUSE, CHURCH STREET 1900 45685

The pace of life at Braunton would have been much the same in 1900 as it was a hundred years earlier. These children could have little realised that they were entering a century unparalleled in history for rapid developments, scientific advances and great wars.

BRAUNTON, NORTH STREET 1900 85686

A 9th-century charter calls Braunton Brannocmynster, in honour of its founding saint. The village was given to Glastonbury Abbey in 857, 'for the taking of salmon'. Large-scale netting of these fish continued until the 20th century, but netting is now a way of life for very few.

BRAUNTON, THE VILLAGE 1900 45687

One person who loved Braunton was John Whittington Ready, rector for some 54 years in the 19th century. That notable churchman must have crossed this square many times during his long and fulfilled life.

BRAUNTON, THE SQUARE 1936 87579
Visitors to North Devon tend to rush through Braunton on their way to Barnstaple and the coast. This is a real pity, for this very large village has much that is of great historic interest and is a thriving community in its own right.

SAUNTON, OLD COTTAGES 1903 49630
To the north of the sandy desert of Braunton Burrows is the village of Saunton, overlooked by some sightseers whose gaze tends to be drawn southwards towards the mouth of the estuary of the Two Rivers and the beaches in between. There has been some unfortunate tourist developments in this area since this photograph was taken, though there are many charming cottages still there.

SAUNTON, ST ANN'S CHURCH AND THE VICARAGE 1912 64537
In the combes and goyles to the east of Saunton is to be found a great variety of our native wildlife, including deer, foxes and badgers, whilst buzzards circle overhead. On the seaward side can be found gulls, terns, kittiwakes and oystercatchers.

SAUNTON, THE SANDS 1920 69405
At about the time that this photograph was taken a young man, battle-weary from the trenches of the First World War, came to live in the nearby village of Georgeham. Henry Williamson immortalised the area in a series of novels including 'The Dream of Fair Women', 'The Pathway' and, of course, 'Tarka the Otter'.

SAUNTON, THE VILLAGE 1940 89042

This view had changed very little since the 1903 photograph was taken, but this was Saunton during the Battle of Britain; it was a countryside of mined beaches, Home Guard patrols and a new sense of importance for the farmers who worked the nearby fields.

SAUNTON, THE SANDS AND THE HOTEL c1955 S65029

These long sandy beaches have always been popular with bathers. Around the middle of the last century a number of large, purpose-built hotels were provided to cater for the tourist boom.

SAUNTON, THE SANDS c1955 S65056
This view looks back over Saunton Sands to the sand dunes of Braunton Burrows and the estuary of the Taw and Torridge. So sandy and extensive are Braunton Burrows that they doubled for the Sahara Desert in the 1945 film 'Caesar and Cleopatra', which starred Claude Rains and Vivien Leigh.

CROYDE, THE BAY 1894 33432
Croyde is an old manor of the parish of Georgeham; it was wonderful scenery such as this which inspired the author Henry Williamson to settle in the locality. Williamson's tall figure was a familiar sight along this coastline as he walked the cliffs and beaches researching his books. He died in 1977 and rests now in the shadow of the church tower at Georgeham.

CROYDE, THE BAY 1912 64543

Another writer who settled near Croyde was the American journalist Negley Farson. This irascible though kind-hearted character was a renowned fisherman, a chronicler of 20th-century events and a noted war correspondent. Farson and Henry Williamson became friends after the Second World War, and seemed to enjoy their periodic feuds.

CROYDE, THE LOOK-OUT TOWER 1912 64546

This is a coastline of lovely views, but few are grander than the vista from the Look-Out Tower at Croyde. Far out in the channel beyond, the Island of Lundy can be seen on clear days.

CROYDE, THE BAY 1912 64542
Two atmospheric views of the coastline at Croyde Bay.

CROYDE, THE BAY 1912 64541A
To see this part of the North Devon coast at its best, and to savour some of the splendour evoked in these photographs, it is a good idea to come and stay out of season, when there are fewer tourists around.

CROYDE, THE BAY AND BAGGY POINT 1936 87583
In the far distance is the prominent headland of Baggy Point, against which the waves crash on stormy winter days. These beaches have now become the preserve of surfers, who bravely ride the white-crested waves ashore.

CROYDE, OLD COTTAGES 1936 87584
Here we see a summer's day in Croyde before there was too much traffic on the roads to distract the eye from the loveliness of the thatched cottages. On the left-hand side of the road is a chapel of ease for parishioners reluctant to make the longer journey to Georgeham church.

CROYDE, THE VILLAGE 1936 87585

CROYDE
The Village 1936
A little girl seeks the welcome shade of a tree on a hot summer's day. Croyde has retained much of its character, despite the huge seasonal increase in population of tourists from the caravan and holiday camps nearby.

CROYDE
The NALGO Holiday Centre c1960
Many trade unions had holiday centres for their members during the earlier years of the 20th century. The camp at Croyde belonged to the National Association of Local Government Officers. A holiday here must have been a welcome break from the world of work.

CROYDE, THE NALGO HOLIDAY CENTRE c1960 C200045

Along the Iron Coast

JUST PAST MORWENSTOW, the walker following the South West Coastal Footpath leaves Cornwall and enters Devon at the parish of Welcombe. But in geographical and scenic terms little changes. The Cornish coastline and this far north-west corner of Devon are not dissimilar. For this is the Iron Coast: harsh and unremitting on stormy days, still treated warily by sailors who regard with caution the high cliffs rising so steeply from the Atlantic Ocean. And there is probably a little voice in every seaman's head reminding him that this was once a wreckers' coast.

Tales are still told of 'Cruel' Coppinger, king of the wreckers, who brought fear and death to this seascape as he lured ships to their doom. How much is fiction as opposed to fact is debatable, for R S Hawker, the eccentric vicar of Morwenstow, and chronicler of Coppinger's misdeeds, was, to say the least, prone to exaggeration. All that is known for certain is that a Daniel Herbert Coppinger was the sole survivor of a ship wrecked at Welcombe Mouth in 1792. He was taken in by a local farmer called William Arthur, but soon abused his host's hospitality. After marrying a local girl, all we know for certain is that Coppinger was declared bankrupt and spent time as a prisoner in the King's Bench gaol in 1802. Where those bare facts end, legend takes over. Locals tell how Coppinger and his gang of ruffians used bright lights to bring ships aground on the rocks and reefs which line this coast. The wrecked ships would be looted, and any

surviving crew members murdered. On one occasion, Coppinger is said to have beheaded a preventative man working for the Customs. This finally brought the wrath of the authorities down on the wrecking enterprise, forcing Coppinger to flee. Retribution was swift and rather ironic. Taking to sea in an open boat, Coppinger was overtaken by a great storm and drowned.

All of this might give the impression that that the Iron Coast is always stark and forbidding. It is not. On calm summer days even its bleakest sections are beautiful; the yellow of the gorse and the green of the turf attracts not wreckers nowadays, but the many ramblers who adore this stretch of the coastal footpath.

The coastline has several large settlements, most of which grew up around the fishing industry or through cross-channel trading with Wales. By popular acclaim the most attractive village is Clovelly. Here the visitor has a real taste of the past, for motor traffic is barred from its streets - cars and coaches are forced to park at the top of its steep hill. The main street is both stepped and cobbled, and goods have long been brought down them using sledges and donkeys. The cottages of Clovelly are chocolate-box pretty, and almost unchanged since the earliest of these photographs was taken. But the real joy of Clovelly is its setting, for the village is surrounded by some of the most beautiful natural scenery in England. Walk along the wooded cliffs in early summer, when the leaves are the freshest shade of green imaginable, and a variety of Devon's birdlife sings to accompany you on your walk. Or come in the autumn, when you will discover just how many shades of brown and gold there really are.

The cliffs of the Iron Coast die away as the estuary of the Taw and Torridge is approached. Long miles of beaches and sand dunes take their place. Here is the resort of Westward Ho!, the only place-name in Britain with an exclamation mark after it. As a settlement it is totally artificial, beginning its existence as recently as 1863. It was named after Charles Kingsley's stirring tale of seafaring folk, a great favourite with Victorian readers, though Kingsley hated the place. Westward Ho! achieved further literary fame when Rudyard Kipling, who was educated at

the United Services College in the resort, used it as a setting for his enduring school story 'Stalky and Co'.

Like most resorts of its kind, people tend either to warm to the atmosphere and surroundings of Westward Ho! or they do not. Its setting is certainly a good one for the holidaymaker who loves to bathe as well as see the sights. To the west is the unspoiled countryside of the Iron Coast, and to the east the great estuary of the Taw and Torridge and the larger towns of Barnstaple and Bideford. For anyone who wishes to combine touring with a traditional seaside holiday, then Westward Ho! is a grand place to stay. Certainly, the people captured for ever in these photographs seem to have been enjoying every minute of their break.

CLOVELLY, LANDING FROM THE STEAMER 1908 61015

HARTLAND
The Quay c1871

Hartland Quay was once a very busy port, created with the support of Sir Francis Drake, Sir Walter Raleigh and other Elizabethan sea dogs. The original quay, shown here, was washed away in the great storms of 1887 and 1896. A new quay was opened in 1979.

HARTLAND
The Village 1929

In Elizabethan days, Hartland was a larger settlement than Bideford. A great abbey was founded here before the Norman Conquest, under the sponsorship of King Harold II's mother, but it has now disappeared. An 18th-century manor occupies the site.

HARTLAND, THE QUAY c1871 5931

HARTLAND, THE VILLAGE 1929 82871

HARTLAND, FORE STREET c1965 H31046

Leland, the traveller and topographer, suggested that Hartland acquired its name from the multitude of stags in the area. The village stands a couple of miles inland from the towering cliffs of Hartland Point.

STOKE, THE VILLAGE 1929 82874

Stoke lies along the road from Hartland to Hartland Quay. Its important perpendicular church and quaint cottages have remained mostly unchanged since this photograph was taken. Tourists nowadays can expect to encounter more than one motor car.

CLOVELLY, THE STREET, LOOKING DOWN c1875 7977
From quite early in Victoria's reign, photographers sought out the steep, picturesque streets of Clovelly as a subject for their work. Even today, no rack of postcards is complete without several pictures of this cliffside village.

CLOVELLY, THE QUAYHEAD c1885 C124501
It is important to remember that even villages now devoted to tourism were once working communities. Clovelly was an important fishing port when this picture was taken. It was not unknown for a single Clovelly boat to bring nine thousand herrings to shore after a single trip.

CLOVELLY, THE STREET 1890 24769
Much of the Clovelly we see today owes its existence to the Cary family, who inherited the village in 1370. As lords of the manor they created the safe little harbour and helped to establish a substantial fleet of fishing vessels.

CLOVELLY, THE HARBOUR 1890 24770
Charles Kingsley, the author of 'Westward Ho!', spent part of his boyhood in this beautiful corner of Devon and used Clovelly as a setting for part of his famous novel. His father was the rector and soon impressed the locals as 'a man who feared no danger, and could steer a boat, hoist and lower a sail, shoot a herring net, and haul a seine as one of themselves'.

Clovelly, The Street, looking Down 1890 24766
No motor traffic is allowed to enter Clovelly's steep and cobbled main street. For generations donkeys and sledges were used to transport goods.

CLOVELLY, MAIN STREET 1894 33490
Notice the sign in advertising 'Views of the Neighbourhood' - some were probably by Frith.

CLOVELLY, THE HARBOUR 1906 55953
A fisherman poses for the camera, with the village in the background. It is interesting to speculate on the tales he might have told Edwardian visitors who sought him out for a yarn.

CLOVELLY, FROM THE BEACH 1908 61006
This photograph gives some idea of the steepness of the hillside on which Clovelly is situated. It was probably its geographical setting that prevented the village from being over-developed.

CLOVELLY, LANDING ON THE QUAY 1908 61014
From Victoria's time the boatmen of Clovelly have taken tourists on sailing ships along the Iron Coast. Winter storms bring great waves crashing against the sturdy sea wall.

CLOVELLY, LANDING FROM THE STEAMER 1908 61015
An Edwardian lady steps elegantly ashore at Clovelly, a boat having brought her inshore from an anchored steamer.
Some visitors have always visited this pretty village by sea from neighbouring ports on calm days.

CLOVELLY
The Harbour and the Red Lion 1935
Amongst early visitors to Clovelly was Charles Dickens, who extolled the joys of the locality, with its woodland walks, wild coastal scenery, and early-blooming roses and fuchsias.

CLOVELLY
The Post Office,
Transferring the Mail 1936
A pre-war mail-van brings the village post to Higher Clovelly, about as far as motor vehicles are allowed to go, where it is transferred to a more practical form of transport. Roy Fisher, the local postman at that time, stands next to the donkey that will accompany him on his delivery.

CLOVELLY, THE HARBOUR AND THE RED LION 1935 86645

CLOVELLY, THE POST OFFICE, TRANSFERRING THE MAIL 1936 87551

CLOVELLY, THE RED LION HOTEL c1960 C124095

CLOVELLY
The Red Lion Hotel c1960
The Red Lion is one of the largest hotels in the locality. The luggage of guests, essential supplies, and even furniture, would have to either negotiate the car-free main street or come by sea.

◆

BUCKS MILLS
The Cliffs 1906
The little hamlet of Bucks Mills made a living from the herring and mackerel fishing, rather like Clovelly. Today it is the haunt of the holiday visitor and the rambler striding out along the coastal footpath.

BUCKS MILLS, THE CLIFFS 1906 55987

BUCKS MILLS, FROM ABOVE 1930 83485

There was a time when nearly every cottage in Bucks Mills was occupied by a member of the Braund family - the elder of the family being the King of Buksh. An ancient rhyme relates how 'The Braunds of Buksh, They swim like ducks, A mighty race are they...'

BUCKS MILLS, THE CLIFFS 1935 86648

The steep climb from the beach at Bucks Mills was built to facilitate the transportation of lime, brought across from Wales. The lime was burned in the local lime-kilns and spread on the nearby fields to neutralise the acid soil.

PARKHAM, THE VILLAGE C1955 P161005

Parkham Church, seen here across a meadow, dates mainly from the 15th century, though parts of the building go back to at least Norman times. The local squire, Lord Halsbury, was Lord Chancellor of England towards the end of Victoria's reign.

PARKHAM, VIEW FROM BUCKLAND ROAD C1955 P161008

Parkham stands a mile or two inland from Bucks Mills, and must have been an isolated settlement centuries ago. Even so, the plague reached here, according to one funereal monument inside the church.

ABBOTSHAM
The Village 1906 55971
It is interesting to wonder what happened to all of the children in this photograph. They must have led a lonely life at Abbotsham at this time - a far cry from the children of today, so familiar with the crowds of tourists who flood in to North Devon.

ABBOTSHAM, THE CHURCH - SOUTH SIDE 1890 24838
Abbotsham's church is an architectural gem, with a magnificent barrel roof over five centuries old. The splendid reredos is a memorial to the son of the vicar in the early 20th century, who was killed like so many others in the First World War.

ABBOTSHAM, THE VILLAGE 1906 55973
Abbotsham, as the name suggests, was part of the endowment of Tavistock Abbey in the 10th century. Here we see a farm labourer returning home from a days work, the sharp prongs of his pitchfork protected by a piece of sacking.

ABBOTSHAM, THE NEW INN c1965 A3233
This view looks back in the opposite direction to photograph No 55973 half a century later. Cars, which would have been a novelty to our farm labourer, now dominate the narrow lanes of North Devon, carrying tourists coming from far afield to sample the delights of the New Inn.

WESTWARD HO!, FROM ABOVE 1899 43082
Eventually the great cliffs of the Iron Coast fall away, bringing us to the sandbanks and low-lying ground of Westward Ho! - the only place-name in the British Isles with an exclamation mark!

WESTWARD HO!, THE PEBBLE RIDGE 1906 55961

WESTWARD HO!
The Pebble Ridge 1906
The shingle beach may keep the sea-water cold, but it certainly helps to protect the low-lying areas around Westward Ho! Here a group of Edwardian young ladies pose somewhat self-consciously for the camera.

◆

WESTWARD HO!
The Pebble Ridge 1912
Westward Ho! owes its name and existence to Charles Kingsley's famous novel - an honour probably unique in Britain. The village began life only in 1863, when Westward Ho! was riding high in the Victorian best-seller lists.

WESTWARD HO!, THE PEBBLE RIDGE 1912 64553

WESTWARD HO!, THE VILLAGE 1919 69354

It is interesting that Charles Kingsley, a Devonian by birth, hated the resort when he visited it. But generations of holidaymakers have enjoyed going there, and Westward Ho! is now a bustling tourist resort of caravan and camping sites.

WESTWARD HO!, THE GOLF LINKS 1920 69360

The level ground around Westward Ho! led to the early creation of a golf course, and here we see an early championship game in progress. Walking, cycling and riding are popular present-day activities here, with yachting and windsurfing attracting those who do not mind getting wet.

WESTWARD HO!, FROM THE EAST 1930 83504
Westward Ho! has found immortality elsewhere in literature, thanks to Rudyard Kipling; he set his school novel 'Stalky and Co' in the resort. Part of the hillside nearby is kept as an open space in memory of the famous novelist and poet.

WESTWARD HO!, THE PROMENADE 1932 85352
Kipling spent his own schooldays here at the United Services College. One of his later poems describes that spartan establishment: 'Twelve bleak houses by the shore, Seven summers by the shore, Mid two hundred brothers.'

WESTWARD HO!, THE PROMENADE 1935 86641

The seas wash across the remains of an ancient forest, dating back to the Late Stone Age. Remains of Neolithic life have been found nearby, such as the bones of domesticated animals and working tools.

WESTWARD HO!, THE SWIMMING POOL 1937 88178

The swimming pool has been easily adapted from the natural rockbeds of the seashore; the water is as cold as the nearby ocean.

Ilfracombe & the Exmoor Coast

AFTER THE SUBTLE landscape of sand and downlands around the estuary of the Taw and Torridge, the North Devon coast regains its height and drama as it approaches Baggy Point and Morte Point. The latter, 'the rock of death', certainly deserves its name and reputation. In one year alone - 1852 - five ships were lost in its shadow. Morte Point is a fearsome sight on dark days when the waves beat the shore and the spray crashes over the headland.

Ilfracombe is the largest resort on the North Devon coast. It is an unusual town, with its buildings scattered across and around a circle of steep pinnacled hills and crags. Much of the town we see today is Victorian or later, its architecture loved or hated in equal measure by visitors and locals. Like so many English resorts, it owes its fortunes to Napoleon Bonaparte. The Emperor's wars closed the Continent to the well-heeled and fashionable visitor just at the time that vacationing was achieving its greatest early popularity. Small fishing and trading ports were eagerly seized upon by these restricted holidaymakers, and by the entrepreneurial spirits that saw a way of making money out of this golden opportunity. Given the drama of the coastline, the sandy beaches, the shelter from bad weather and the picturesque 'sights' all around, Ilfracombe fitted the bill very nicely.

But look closely under the surface, and there is a great deal of evidence of an older settlement. The manor of Ilfracombe is very ancient, having belonged at one time or another to some of the greatest of English families, such as the Champernownes, the Audleys, the Bourchiers and Sir Philip Sidney. It was the Bourchiers who built the pier and enlarged it in 1829. In earlier times this little port had contributed six ships for the fleet of Edward III, then at war with France. In 1644, during the English Civil War, the town witnessed conflict when it was captured by Sir Francis Doddington's cavalry.

Ilfracombe's fortunes were mixed during the 20th century, with its prosperity declining as traditional family holidays came to an end. But towards the end of that troubled century there was a rebirth, with short-break visitors coming once again to the town. A new theatre, the Landmark, has been built right by the sea, offering year-round entertainment; Ilfracombe has also become a floral area of excellence, regularly winning the Britain in Bloom competition. Photographers who wish to copy a little bit of the old Frith magic would do well to visit Ilfracombe in June, when the town holds its annual Victorian celebrations. Local people dress up in Victorian costume and can be seen wandering along the front and around the shops - a Frith street scene brought to life.

Combe Martin, just down the coast, boasts a main street of a couple of miles in length, and lies just outside the western boundary of the Exmoor National Park. This sheltered valley was famous for its silver mines in past times, and its prosperity helped to fund the Hundred Years' War. Traces of the old mines can be found in and around the valley. The best example is right opposite the village church; some of the mine tunnels must have run right under the village street. From Victorian times, this deep and sheltered valley became a haven for market gardeners. No wonder, for on hot days the combe proves to be a very efficient sun trap, well-protected from the Atlantic's westerly gales that batter the most exposed portions of this coast.

A walk along the coastal path eastwards from Combe Martin takes the walker to the huge hilltops of Little and Great Hangman, the westernmost giants of Exmoor. This scenery, where the highlands of the hill-district drop suddenly to the ocean, has to be some of the most spectacular in England. The cliffs are high, and apart from a few inlets, form a considerable barrier against the sea. Apart from a few hamlets, the coast is wild and lonely all the way to Lynton and Lynmouth.

The first of these two towns is fairly functional, Victorian in appearance, and certainly not the most attractive along the coast. But many have loved it. Sir George Newnes, the publisher of popular magazines, was its benefactor in a multitude of ways. A compassionate man, he hated the sight of horses struggling up the steep hill from Lynmouth, so he instigated the building of the present cliff railway to relieve them of their burdens.

In 1952, the tributaries of the River Lyn, which together drain much of the Exmoor watershed, came together and devastated the little town of Lynmouth. Many died, and a considerable number of buildings were destroyed or damaged. This makes the photographs that follow an invaluable record of the earlier town, as it might have been seen by the Romantic poets, such as Coleridge, Wordsworth and Shelley. The setting of Lynmouth was well described by the Poet Laureate of that period, Robert Southey, as '...a view beautiful enough to repay the weariness of a long journey; but to complete it, there is the blue and boundless sea'. Many a visitor to Lynmouth will echo the poet's sentiments.

Woolacombe, The Village 1895 35886
Dramatic clifftops and sweeping sands make the coastline around Woolacombe a delight for the visitor who loves wild countryside. Out to sea, the island of Lundy rides the ocean like a ship, and the sea sings as it reaches the shore.

WOOLACOMBE, THE VILLAGE 1899 43130

Woolacombe has grown in size considerably since this photograph was taken just over a century ago, transforming the then village into a bustling holiday resort. The cliff path takes in the prominent headlands of Morte Point and Baggy Head, with five miles of glorious sand stretching between.

WOOLACOMBE, SHELL BEACH 1911 63942

As the posture of a few of the people in this photograph suggests, these local beaches have always attracted the attentions of the amateur conchologist. Coins from wrecked ships are also sometimes found - a reminder of the dangers of this coastline.

WOOLACOMBE
On the Clifftop 1911

This was once a wreckers' coast, with many a ship being lured to its doom on the rocks and long stretches of sand. It is said that the beaches here are haunted by one ship's captain who was washed ashore alive, but held under the water until he drowned.

◆

MORTEHOE
Barricane Beach c1885

Barricane Beach is an excellent location for the seeker of shells thanks to its peculiar geography, which allows the tides to trap them there. It is easily visited by walking the coastal footpath between Woolacombe and Mortehoe.

WOOLACOMBE, ON THE CLIFFTOP 1911 63938

MORTEHOE, BARRICANE BEACH c1885 M99503

MORTEHOE, MORTE POINT FROM BULL POINT c1900 M99504
Morte Point, as its name suggests, has seen the end of many sailing vessels and the death of their crews. But it is an exhilarating place to visit on a stormy day, and a good place to watch the sun set when the weather is calm. It now belongs to the National Trust.

MORTEHOE, THE VILLAGE c1900 M99501
Mortehoe seems to have grown out of the very rocky headlands on which it is situated. It is a windswept place on stormy days, but a sun-trap in the summer when the breeze has died away.

MORTEHOE, THE LIGHTHOUSE, BULL POINT c1900 M99502

The lighthouse and foghorn of Bull Point were familiar to generations of seafaring folk. The coastline here can be harsh and unforgiving to those in trouble at sea - but beautiful and dramatic to those people who enjoy wild scenery.

MORTEHOE, GENERAL VIEW 1935 87127

Mortehoe is a much older place than neighbouring Woolacombe, though both now exist mostly for tourism. This corner of North Devon can be quite busy on hot summer days, but retains its old loneliness for the benefit of the off-season visitor.

MORTEHOE, GENERAL VIEW 1935 87128
To cater for the tourist trade, many of the buildings on the coastal side of Mortehoe are now hotels. This stretch of the coastal footpath and the wild countryside inland make Mortehoe an ideal holiday location for the hardier rambler.

MORTEHOE, THE CHURCH 1935 87130
It is said that one tomb inside Mortehoe church holds the bones of William de Tracey, one of the four murderers of Thomas Becket, though some historians have cast doubt upon the tale. What is certain is that the de Traceys held land in the area at around this period.

LEE, THE CLIFFS AND BULL POINT 1890 22965
The South West Coastal Footpath winds around the West Country peninsula from Poole in Dorset to Minehead in Somerset, traversing some of the most beautiful scenery in the British Isles.

LEE, THE VALLEY 1899 43124
In a sheltered combe, just as the coast path turns eastwards towards Ilfracombe, is the delightful village of Lee. It is always a great favourite with visitors because of its romantic and wooded setting.

LEE, THE CLIFFS 1937 88190
Given the wild and rugged nature of the coast, the earliest inhabitants of Lee were fortunate indeed to find such a sheltered valley in which to make their homes - a far cry from the wind-blown settlements elsewhere along the coast.

LEE, THE VILLAGE 1937 88196
Some of the cottages at Lee date back to the 16th century, and are picturesque in comparison to the sturdier dwellings on the clifftops. But then they have the benefit of shelter from the fierce Atlantic gales.

LEE, THE THREE OLD MAIDS COTTAGE 1937 88197

One of the most attractive cottages in Lee is the former home of the famous three spinsters who lived here for many years. When this photograph was taken, the cottage housed a collection of dresses from earlier times.

LEE, THE POST OFFICE c1965 L27049

Villagers halt for a chat on the way to the post office, always an important meeting place for any Devon community. The luxuriant growth of flowers and bushes gives some idea of how sheltered Lee is when compared to the higher coastal ground.

LEE, THE BEACH c1965 L27064

LEE, THE VILLAGE c1965 L27091

LEE
The Beach c1965

Visitors to Lee pose for the photographer as they await a boat trip along the coast. The beach at Lee may be rocky in places, but it still attracts bathers.

LEE
The Village c1965

Tourists who are fond of small resorts would do well to spend their holiday at Lee. When the day-trippers have gone back to neighbouring Ilfracombe, Lee becomes as quiet as it must have been in earlier times.

LEE, LAUNCHING THE BOATS c1965 L27093

It is quite likely that fishermen have set off from this cove for over a thousand years. The boats are small, and used for handlining and collecting lobsters, but are quite capable of coping with a rough swell. Boat trips for tourists became a useful sideline in the 20th century.

ILFRACOMBE, THE HARBOUR c1890 I50001

Ilfracombe was a market town until the Napoleonic Wars closed the Continent to tourism. The rocky coastline, slate cliffs and steep hillsides give Ilfracombe its distinctive appearance.

ILFRACOMBE, THE PIER 1899 43117

Ilfracombe's harbour, well-protected from the often wild sea beyond, led to the town's development as a small port.
On Lantern Hill stands one of the strangest of all lighthouses. It was originally a chapel dedicated to St Nicholas.
A lantern was displayed to guide early fishermen.

ILFRACOMBE, CAPSTONE HILL AND THE PARADE 1911 63901

In 1797 four French ships sank several English vessels off the North Devon coast. As the men of Ilfracombe were
away at the war, the town's ladies draped their red petticoats over their shoulders and took up prominent positions.
The French, imagining they were facing an army of redcoats, sailed away.

ILFRACOMBE, FROM CAPSTONE HILL 1911 63905

Ilfracombe's architecture is predominantly Victorian, and has changed little since this photograph was taken in the first year of George V's reign. Despite this relatively modern look, its church was begun by the Normans and its manorial records date back nearly as far.

ILFRACOMBE 1923 74948

Ilfracombe's fortunes declined in the late 20th century as the traditional seaside holiday came to an end. The town has, however, revived somewhat with the introduction of short-break and touring vacations. These holidaymakers were obviously enjoying their break in the resort.

BERRYNARBOR, GENERAL VIEW 1934 86451

Berrynarbor gets its name from the Berry family, whose ancient manor adjoins the 15th-century church. In the churchyard lies Richard Turpie, a sailor of great renown, who explored the islands of the Pacific on behalf of the London Missionary Society. He once survived many days in an open boat after his ship foundered.

BERRYNARBOR, THE VILLAGE C1960 B73019

John Jewel, the Elizabethan bishop of Salisbury, was born in the parish of Berrynarbor. His defence of Protestantism, 'Apologia pro Ecclesia Anglicana', written in 1562, was ordered to be read in every church in the land by Elizabeth I.

BERRYNARBOR
Sterridge Valley c1960
The scenery around Berrynarbor has a pastoral quality. Notice the horse and trap in the lane, a rare form of transport in the 1960s, which gives this scene a quite timeless feel.

◆

BERRYNARBOR
The Village c1965
Here we have a fine view over Berrynarbor, a typical Devon hilltop village. Despite an increase in traffic, the villages of the North Coast are still delightful places to live.

BERRYNARBOR, STERRIDGE VALLEY c1960 B73011

BERRYNARBOR, THE VILLAGE c1965 B73050

BERRYNARBOR, THE BAY AND WATERMOUTH VALLEY c1960 B73020
A pleasant walk from Berrynarbor towards the sea brings us to Watermouth Castle, an attractive property built as late as 1825. Local tradition alleges that a battlemented castle stood on this site in the Middle Ages.

COMBE MARTIN, GENERAL VIEW 1911 63957
Combe Martin must have one of the longest village streets in England. This thoroughfare stretches for over a mile down the length of this deep valley leading down to the sea. The church is half way down the street, with the harbour at the far northern end.

COMBE MARTIN, THE HARBOUR 1911 63963
This old village gets its name from the Norman baron Martyn de Tours. The bay is tightly shut in by rocks, and was converted into a more practical harbour during Victoria's reign. It is still used by yachts and fishing boats.

COMBE MARTIN, THE STRAND 1926 79236
Combe Martin has had a long reputation for its silver and lead mines, which have been worked sporadically since the time of Edward I. It is said that these natural riches helped to defray the costs of England's participation in the Hundred Years' War.

COMBE MARTIN, A SCHOONER IN THE HARBOUR 1935 86745

A Victorian commentator noted that 'the pebbles of the beach are burnt into lime; and laver is gathered at low tide and eaten in some quantity by the poor of the village'. This is a reminder that life in Devon's villages was not always a rural idyll.

COMBE MARTIN, FROM ABOVE 1930 83463

The tower of Combe Martin's church is over a hundred feet tall, and dominates the centre of the village. Its attractive appearance gained it a mention in an old local rhyme about churches: 'Hartland for length, Berrynarbor for strength, Combe Martin for beauty'.

COMBE MARTIN, SEASIDE HILL 1930 83456
Combe Martin lies in the midst of very good country for walking. The rambler is spoiled for choice, having not only the coastal paths and the sites of the old mines to explore, but the very western edge of the Exmoor National Park.

PARRACOMBE, FROM FAIRFIELD 1907 59438
An excursion inland to take in some of the delights of western Exmoor brings us to Parracombe. Its two churches, one Norman and the other Victorian, can both be seen in this photograph.

PARRACOMBE, THE VILLAGE 1907 59422

Parracombe lies amidst some of the highest ground in the district: the hills rise to over 1500 feet around the village. The area is rich in history, with Bronze Age barrows dotted across Parracombe Common, and a good array of medieval farmsteads nearby.

PARRACOMBE, THE OLD CHURCH OF ST PETROCK 1907 59444

This beautiful old church dates back to Norman times, and is one of the joys of North Devon with its unspoiled Georgian interior. Astonishingly, there were plans to demolish the building in the 1870s, but it was saved from destruction thanks to the endeavours of Victorian conservationists, including John Ruskin.

PARRACOMBE, THE OLD POST OFFICE c1955 P11026
Christianity came early to Parracombe. 1500 years ago Saint Petrock came here and built a chapel of cob and wattle. This was superseded by the later Norman church.

PARRACOMBE, THE VILLAGE STREET c1955 P11027
A second church was built in Parracombe in 1878, to cope with the growing population. The more ancient church of St Petrock is still used occasionally for services, and both buildings are worth a visit.

BARBROOK, CHERRY BRIDGE 1907 59424
Cherry Bridge lies by a quiet lane leading to some of the remotest countryside on Exmoor. Eventually, the lane peters out on Thornworthy Common - only walkers and riders can go further.

BARBROOK, THE VILLAGE 1935 86631
Barbrook straddles the West Lyn River, just as its swirling waters enter one last wooded combe before reaching the sea at Lynmouth. Many motorists rush through Barbrook in their hurry to reach the coast, which is a real pity; there are several attractive walks in the neighbourhood.

BARBROOK, BEGGARS ROOST 1935 86632
Beggars Roost is situated on the hillside between Barbrook and the higher ground around Windypost Cross and Lyn Down. This is a pleasant way to stroll down to Lynmouth using footpaths and bridleways instead of the busy main road.

LYNTON, LEE BAY 1920 69390
The metamorphic rocks of Lee Bay provide an exciting backdrop for the coastal traveller journeying eastwards towards Lynton and Lynmouth. These cliffs, where the high hills of Exmoor drop suddenly to the sea, are some of the most spectacular in England.

LYNTON, THE VALLEY OF THE ROCKS 1907 59384
It is believed that the Valley of the Rocks was created during the last Ice Age. It is now a wild landscape of crags and pinnacles, occupied by a famous herd of wild goats. On a clear day the mountains of Wales can be seen.

LYNTON, THE VALLEY OF THE ROCKS HOTEL 1907 59372
The stagecoach 'Defiance' was owned by Mr T Copp; it used to give Edwardian tourists an exciting taste of earlier times as it made its way along the coastal roads of Exmoor. Even a century ago, stagecoaches were something of an anachronism.

LYNTON, THE STAGECOACH 1911 63828

LYNTON
The Stagecoach 1911
A stagecoach halts outside Lynton church. Lynton is mostly a Victorian and Edwardian town - even the 13th-century church tower has suffered from rebuilding during those periods. However, it is an excellent base for the exploration of Exmoor.

LYNTON
From Above c1965
Lynton gained a great deal from the patronage of the publisher Sir George Newnes, who loved the place. It was he who instigated the building of the cliff railway up from Lynmouth, because he hated the sight of horses struggling up the steep hill between the two towns. Lynton's benefactor lies buried in the town he loved so much.

LYNTON, FROM ABOVE C1965 L127074

LYNMOUTH, THE PIER 1899 43095

Lynmouth became a popular resort during the war with Napoleon. Amongst early visitors were the poets Robert Southey and Percy Bysshe Shelley. The latter spent his honeymoon here with his teenage bride Harriet Westbrook. Tradition alleges that Shelley was spied upon by government agents, who considered him a dangerous revolutionary and subversive.

LYNMOUTH, THE VILLAGE 1907 59397

The Poet Laureate Robert Southey was full of praise for the delights of Lynmouth. He remarked '...a view beautiful enough to repay the weariness of a long journey; but to complete it, there is the blue and boundless sea'.

LYNMOUTH, THE EAST AND WEST LYN 1911 63855

On the night of 15 August 1952, a storm swelled the waters of the Lyn and its many tributaries, flooding the town. Thirty-one people died, and ninety-three houses were destroyed. Lynmouth was changed for ever from the placid scene we see here.

LYNMOUTH, THE VILLAGE 1920 69366

The River Lyn is now enclosed between high, banked walls to prevent a repetition of that dreadful night. Many of the buildings seen here were lost in the great flood, but the beauty of Lynmouth's setting still remains.

COUNTISBURY, THE BLUE BALL INN 1907 59406
A road climbs eastwards from Lynmouth and brings the traveller to the tiny village of Countisbury.

COUNTISBURY, THE BLUE BALL INN 1929 82248
In these two photographs we see two very different forms of transport - but both were designed to convey their passengers along the very best parts of the North Devon Coast.

Index

Frith Book Co Titles

Frith Book Company publish over a 100 new titles each year. For latest catalogue please contact Frith Book Co.

Town Books 96pp, 100 photos. County and Themed Books 128pp, 150 photos (unless specified) All titles hardback laminated case and jacket except those indicated pb (paperback)

Title	ISBN	Price
Around Barnstaple	1-85937-084-5	£12.99
Around Blackpool	1-85937-049-7	£12.99
Around Bognor Regis	1-85937-055-1	£12.99
Around Bristol	1-85937-050-0	£12.99
Around Cambridge	1-85937-092-6	£12.99
Cheshire	1-85937-045-4	£14.99
Around Chester	1-85937-090-X	£12.99
Around Chesterfield	1-85937-071-3	£12.99
Around Chichester	1-85937-089-6	£12.99
Cornwall	1-85937-054-3	£14.99
Cotswolds	1-85937-099-3	£14.99
Around Derby	1-85937-046-2	£12.99
Devon	1-85937-052-7	£14.99
Dorset	1-85937-075-6	£14.99
Dorset Coast	1-85937-062-4	£14.99
Around Dublin	1-85937-058-6	£12.99
East Anglia	1-85937-059-4	£14.99
Around Eastbourne	1-85937-061-6	£12.99
English Castles	1-85937-078-0	£14.99
Around Falmouth	1-85937-066-7	£12.99
Hampshire	1-85937-064-0	£14.99
Isle of Man	1-85937-065-9	£14.99
Around Maidstone	1-85937-056-X	£12.99
North Yorkshire	1-85937-048-9	£14.99
Around Nottingham	1-85937-060-8	£12.99
Around Penzance	1-85937-069-1	£12.99
Around Reading	1-85937-087-X	£12.99
Around St Ives	1-85937-068-3	£12.99
Around Salisbury	1-85937-091-8	£12.99
Around Scarborough	1-85937-104-3	£12.99
Scottish Castles	1-85937-077-2	£14.99
Around Sevenoaks and Tonbridge	1-85937-057-8	£12.99
Sheffield and S Yorkshire	1-85937-070-5	£14.99
Shropshire	1-85937-083-7	£14.99
Staffordshire	1-85937-047-0 (96pp)	£12.99
Suffolk	1-85937-074-8	£14.99
Surrey	1-85937-081-0	£14.99
Around Torbay	1-85937-063-2	£12.99
Wiltshire	1-85937-053-5	£14.99
Around Bakewell	1-85937-113-2	£12.99
Around Bournemouth	1-85937-067-5	£12.99
Cambridgeshire	1-85937-086-1	£14.99
Essex	1-85937-082-9	£14.99
Around Great Yarmouth	1-85937-085-3	£12.99
Hertfordshire	1-85937-079-9	£14.99
Isle of Wight	1-85937-114-0	£14.99
Around Lincoln	1-85937-111-6	£12.99
Oxfordshire	1-85937-076-4	£14.99
Around Shrewsbury	1-85937-110-8	£12.99
South Devon Coast	1-85937-107-8	£14.99
Around Stratford upon Avon	1-85937-098-5	£12.99
West Midlands	1-85937-109-4	£14.99

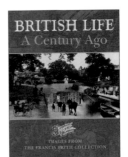

British Life A Century Ago
246 x 189mm
144pp, hardback.
Black and white
Lavishly illustrated with photos from the turn of the century, and with extensive commentary. It offers a unique insight into the social history and heritage of bygone Britain.

1-85937-103-5 £17.99

Available from your local bookshop or from the publisher

Around Bath	1-85937-097-7	£12.99	Mar
Cumbria	1-85937-101-9	£14.99	Mar
Down the Thames	1-85937-121-3	£14.99	Mar
Around Exeter	1-85937-126-4	£12.99	Mar
Greater Manchester	1-85937-108-6	£14.99	Mar
Around Harrogate	1-85937-112-4	£12.99	Mar
Around Leicester	1-85937-073-x	£12.99	Mar
Around Liverpool	1-85937-051-9	£12.99	Mar
Northumberland and Tyne & Wear			
	1-85937-072-1	£14.99	Mar
Around Oxford	1-85937-096-9	£12.99	Mar
Around Plymouth	1-85937-119-1	£12.99	Mar
Around Southport	1-85937-106-x	£12.99	Mar
Welsh Castles	1-85937-120-5	£14.99	Mar
Canals and Waterways	1-85937-129-9	£17.99	Apr
Around Guildford	1-85937-117-5	£12.99	Apr
Around Horsham	1-85937-127-2	£12.99	Apr
Around Ipswich	1-85937-133-7	£12.99	Apr
Ireland (pb)	1-85937-181-7	£9.99	Apr
London (pb)	1-85937-183-3	£9.99	Apr
New Forest	1-85937-128-0	£14.99	Apr
Around Newark	1-85937-105-1	£12.99	Apr
Around Newquay	1-85937-140-x	£12.99	Apr
Scotland (pb)	1-85937-182-5	£9.99	Apr
Around Southampton	1-85937-088-8	£12.99	Apr
Sussex (pb)	1-85937-184-1	£9.99	Apr
Around Winchester	1-85937-139-6	£12.99	Apr
Around Belfast	1-85937-094-2	£12.99	May
Colchester (pb)	1-85937-188-4	£8.99	May
Exmoor	1-85937-132-9	£14.99	May
Leicestershire (pb)	1-85937-185-x	£9.99	May
Lincolnshire	1-85937-135-3	£14.99	May
North Devon Coast	1-85937-146-9	£14.99	May
Nottinghamshire (pb)	1-85937-187-6	£9.99	May
Peak District	1-85937-100-0	£14.99	May
Around Truro	1-85937-147-7	£12.99	May
Yorkshire (pb)	1-85937-186-8	£9.99	May

Berkshire (pb)	1-85937-191-4	£9.99	Jun
Brighton (pb)	1-85937-192-2	£8.99	Jun
County Durham	1-85937-123-x	£14.99	Jun
Dartmoor	1-85937-145-0	£14.99	Jun
Down the Severn	1-85937-118-3	£14.99	Jun
East London	1-85937-080-2	£14.99	Jun
East Sussex	1-85937-130-2	£14.99	Jun
Glasgow (pb)	1-85937-190-6	£8.99	Jun
Kent (pb)	1-85937-189-2	£9.99	Jun
Kent Living Memories	1-85937-125-6	£14.99	Jun
Redhill to Reigate	1-85937-137-x	£12.99	Jun
Stone Circles & Ancient Monuments			
	1-85937-143-4	£17.99	Jun
Victorian & Edwardian Kent			
	1-85937-149-3	£14.99	Jun
Victorian & Edwardian Maritime Album			
	1-85937-144-2	£17.99	Jun
Victorian & Edwardian Yorkshire			
	1-85937-154-x	£14.99	Jun
West Sussex	1-85937-148-5	£14.99	Jun
Churches of Berkshire	1-85937-170-1	£17.99	Jul
Churches of Dorset	1-85937-172-8	£17.99	Jul
Derbyshire (pb)	1-85937-196-5	£9.99	Jul
Edinburgh (pb)	1-85937-193-0	£8.99	Jul
Folkstone	1-85937-124-8	£12.99	Jul
Gloucestershire	1-85937-102-7	£14.99	Jul
Herefordshire	1-85937-174-4	£14.99	Jul
North London	1-85937-206-6	£14.99	Jul
Norwich (pb)	1-85937-194-9	£8.99	Jul
Ports and Harbours	1-85937-208-2	£17.99	Jul
Somerset and Avon	1-85937-153-1	£14.99	Jul
South Devon Living Memories			
	1-85937-168-x	£14.99	Jul
Warwickshire (pb)	1-85937-203-1	£9.99	Jul
Worcestershire	1-85937-152-3	£14.99	Jul
Yorkshire Living Memories			
	1-85937-166-3	£14.99	Jul

FRITH PRODUCTS & SERVICES

Francis Frith would doubtless be pleased to know that the pioneering publishing venture he started in 1860 still continues today. More than a hundred and thirty years later, The Francis Frith Collection continues in the same innovative tradition and is now one of the foremost publishers of vintage photographs in the world. Some of the current activities include:

Interior Decoration

Today Frith's photographs can be seen framed and as giant wall murals in thousands of pubs, restaurants, hotels, banks, retail stores and other public buildings throughout the country. In every case they enhance the unique local atmosphere of the places they depict and provide reminders of gentler days in an increasingly busy and frenetic world.

Product Promotions

Frith products have been used by many major companies to promote the sales of their own products or to reinforce their own history and heritage. Brands include Hovis bread, Courage beers, Scots Porage Oats, Colman's mustard, Cadbury's foods, Mellow Birds coffee, Dunhill pipe tobacco, Guinness, and Bulmer's Cider.

Genealogy and Family History

As the interest in family history and roots grows world-wide, more and more people are turning to Frith's photographs of Great Britain for images of the towns, villages and streets where their ancestors lived; and, of course, photographs of the churches and chapels where their ancestors were christened, married and buried are an essential part of every genealogy tree and family album.

A series of easy-to-use CD Roms is planned for publication, and an increasing number of Frith photographs will be able to be viewed on specialist genealogy sites. A growing range of Frith books will be available on CD.

The Internet

Already thousands of Frith photographs can be viewed and purchased on the internet. By the end of the year 2000 some 60,000 Frith photographs will be available on the internet. The number of sites is constantly expanding, each focussing on different products and services from the Collection.

Some of the sites are listed below.

www.townpages.co.uk
www.icollector.com
www.barclaysquare.co.uk
www.cornwall-online.co.uk

For background information on the Collection look at the three following sites:

www.francisfrith.com
www.francisfrith.co.uk
www.frithbook.co.uk

Frith Products

All Frith photographs are available Framed or just as Mounted Prints, and can be ordered from the address below. From time to time other products - Address Books, Calendars, Table Mats, etc - are available.

For further information:
if you would like further information on any of the above aspects of the Frith business please contact us at the address below:
The Francis Frith Collection,
Frith's Barn, Teffont, Salisbury, Wiltshire,
England SP3 5QP.
Tel: +44 (0)1722 716 376 Fax: +44 (0)1722 716 881 Email: uksales@francisfrith.com

To receive your FREE Mounted Print

Mounted Print
Overall size 14 x 11 inches

Cut out this Voucher and return it with your remittance for £1.50 to cover postage and handling. Choose any photograph included in this book. Your SEPIA print will be A4 in size, and mounted in a cream mount with burgundy rule lines, overall size 14 x 11 inches.

Order additional Mounted Prints at HALF PRICE (only £7.49 each*)

If there are further pictures you would like to order, possibly as gifts for friends and family, acquire them at half price (no additional postage and handling required).

Have your Mounted Prints framed*

For an additional £14.95 per print you can have your chosen Mounted Print framed in an elegant polished wood and gilt moulding, overall size 16 x 13 inches (no additional postage and handling required).

---

* IMPORTANT!
These special prices are only available if ordered using the original voucher on this page (no copies permitted) and at the same time as your free Mounted Print, for delivery to the same address

---

Frith Collectors' Guild

From time to time we publish a magazine of news and stories about Frith photographs and further special offers of Frith products. If you would like 12 months FREE membership, please return this form.

Send completed forms to:
The Francis Frith Collection, Frith's Barn, Teffont, Salisbury, Wiltshire SP3 5QP

Voucher for FREE and Reduced Price Frith Prints

Picture no.	Page number	Qty	Mounted @ £7.49	Framed + £14.95	Total Cost
		1	**Free of charge***	£	£
			£7.49	£	£
			£7.49	£	£
			£7.49	£	£
			£7.49	£	£
			£7.49	£	£
			* Post & handling		£1.50
Book Title			**Total Order Cost**		£

Please do not photocopy this voucher. Only the original is valid, so please cut it out and return it to us.

I enclose a cheque / postal order for £ . . . . made payable to 'The Francis Frith Collection'
OR please debit my Mastercard / Visa / Switch / Amex card

Number . . . .

Expires . . . . Signature . . . .

Name Mr/Mrs/Ms . . . .

Address . . . .

. . . .

. . . .

. . . . Postcode . . . .

Daytime Tel No . . . . Valid to 31/12/01

The Francis Frith Collectors' Guild

Please enrol me as a member for 12 months free of charge.

Name Mr/Mrs/Ms . . . .

Address . . . .

. . . .

. . . .

. . . . Postcode . . . .

Free Print - see overleaf